THE WIT AND HUMOUR OF WILLIAM HAGUE

Dr. Eileen Metcalfe

authorHOUSE®

AuthorHouse™ UK
1663 Liberty Drive
Bloomington, IN 47403 USA
www.authorhouse.co.uk
Phone: 0800.197.4150

Published by AuthorHouse   01/28/2019

ISBN: 978-1-7283-8394-1 (sc)
ISBN: 978-1-7283-8393-4 (e)

From quiet homes and first beginning,
Out to the undiscovered ends,
There's nothing worth the wear of winning,
But laughter and the love of friends.

Hilaire Belloc

THIS BOOK DEALS WITH THE JOVIAL WIT and humour of William Hague, now Baron Hague of Richmond, taken largely from his speeches and debates in the House of Commons.

It is an informal, lighthearted look at his contribution to political debate made inside the House of Commons. His stand-alone, witty comments quoted here are largely self-explanatory.

These contributions are not given in chronological order but rather on the nature of their impact.

It has been said that nothing describes a man better than his own sense of humour. William Hague's keenly developed sense of humour and penetrating wit is a delightful facet of his personality. Few men in public life display such wit in speeches and comments.

A synopsis: wit, oratory and evasion – a master debater at work.

William Hague was a Member of Parliament for Richmond in North Yorkshire from 1989 until 2015.

He was also:

Secretary of State for Wales 1995–1997

Leader of the Opposition 1997–2001

Shadow Foreign Secretary 2005–2010

Secretary of State for Foreign and Commonwealth Affairs 2010–2014

Leader of the House of Commons 2014–2015

He joined the Conservative Party on his fifteenth birthday and within twelve months he made national news headlines in an unforgettable speech, addressing the Conservatives at their 1977 Annual National Conference.

He got a standing ovation and inspired Margaret Thatcher to call him possibly another younger Pitt.

Hague's name was first mentioned in the House of Commons in January 1989 when Dennis Skinner, with uncharacteristic wit, deliberately held up proceedings (filibustering, i.e. talking out the measure) by trying to move a writ for a by-election in the constituency of Richmond, Yorkshire. David Tredinnick gave a plug to his party as he referred to the superb prospective Conservative candidate, William Hague.

Hansard: Reproduced by permission of the Controller of Her Majesty's Stationery Office.

WILLIAM HAGUE WAS BORN IN ROTHERHAM, YORKSHIRE and educated in Wath-upon-Dearne Comprehensive School. He studied PPE (Politics, Philosophy and Economics) at Magdalen College Oxford, graduating with a First Class Honours degree. He was president of both the Oxford Union and the Oxford University Conservative Association. He went on to study for a Master of Business Administration degree at the business school INSEAD near Paris – the closest Europe gets to Harvard Business School. He then worked as a management consultant at McKinsey & Company where Archie Norman was his mentor.

He was elected to Parliament in a by-election as a Member for Richmond, North Yorkshire in 1989 aged 28 years. Following his election he was the youngest Conservative MP. He became part of the government in 1990, serving as Parliamentary Private Secretary for the then Chancellor of the Exchequer Norman Lamont. In 1993 Hague moved to the Department for Social Security where he was Parliamentary under-Secretary of State. The following year he was promoted to Minister of State at the

Department for Social Security with responsibility for Social Security and Disabled People. His fast rise up through the government is attributed to his skills in debate.

He entered the cabinet in 1995 as Secretary of State for Wales. He made a good impression at the Welsh Office. An astute politician, with a natural sense of humour, he avoided John Redwood's mistake of attempting to mime the Welsh national anthem at a public event. Hague asked a Welsh Office civil servant, Ffion Jenkins, to teach him the words. They married relatively soon after meeting.

He continued serving in the Cabinet until the Conservatives were removed from power in the 1997 general election. Following this defeat, at the age of 36, Hague was elected as the leader of the Conservative Party, in succession to John Major, defeating more experienced politicians such as Kenneth Clarke and Michael Howard. This was, to some extent, a poisoned chalice as when a party has been in power for many years they get blame for what is seen as wrong but do not get due credit for successes. His success was too early.

He was leader from 1997 to 2001. He resigned as party leader after the 2001 general election defeat to the Labour Party.

On the back benches, Hague began a career as an author, writing biographies of William Pitt the Younger and William Wilberforce. He also held several directorships and worked as a consultant and public speaker. Hague's personal popularity both in the Conservative Party and with the wider public can be attributed in great part to his detailed knowledge of all aspects of politics that had fallen into his brief and to his incomparable wit and humour which emerges when least expected but is now generally expected.

He was an active media personality. He put in three much praised appearances as a guest host on the BBC satirical news show *Have I Got News for You*. He is one of the UK's most popular after-dinner speakers. His annual income was one of the highest in Parliament, with earnings from directorships, consultancies, speeches and his parliamentary salary. However, politics was his passion and he dropped several commitments and is estimated to have taken a salary cut of some £600,000 on becoming Shadow Foreign Secretary in 2005. In the 2005 Conservative leadership election he backed the eventual winner David Cameron. Hague was then offered and accepted the role of Shadow Foreign Secretary.

Even after twenty years in politics Hague retains his youthful looks and appeal. Little snippets of comments add to this image: that he was bottle-fed sherry and that he was reading Hansard in his pram. These presumably relate to his boast as a young man that he could drink fourteen pints and to his vast and detailed knowledge of Parliamentary affairs.

William Hague represented a rural constituency in Richmond, North Yorkshire. In his maiden speech he refers to the well-known TV series *Heartbeat*, and to Catterick and RAF Leeming in his constituency. At the end of what was a serious and studied speech he introduces a light touch and a hint of things to come:

"I thank the House for its indulgence and hope that there will be many more occasions, Madam Deputy Speaker, on which I may try to catch your eye."

From the beginning Hague mastered his brief in support of farmers as is testified in his thorough and detailed speeches. Towards the end of a very long, detailed and comprehensive speech in support of farmers Hague complains about how the BBC has aided the hysteria surrounding bovine spongiform encephalopathy (BSE) by showing, "library footage of a cow against other footage of Northallerton in my constituency. That footage of a beast with BSE has appeared hundreds of times and given the impression that BSE is to be found passing through Northallerton market. There is no evidence that such an animal has been through that market, but the footage has now appeared on the BBC more often than Terry Wogan and it is time to stop it."

On another occasion he speaks about poor radio reception in the Yorkshire Dales, also in his constituency. He complains that it is not possible to get the FM signal of BBC radio stations, particularly in Upper Swaledale. He says that the BBC's response to local residents is infuriating. He continues, "It is senseless to ask people in areas such as Swaledale to purchase multi-element aerials and FM radio sets if the signal is absent or too weak to be of value: when nothing is multiplied by something, the answer is still nothing."

Referring to the correspondence with the director general of the BBC that 98 per cent of the population is served by FM radio despite deficiency of FM coverage in Richmond and without FM radio in Swaledale, he concludes:

"Let me provide an analogy. Let us suppose that my hon. and learned Friend and I go into a restaurant where there is a fixed-price menu, and are told that at our table most items on the menu are about to be taken off indefinitely, and one course to be omitted altogether. On inquiring why, we are told that the reason is to allow a better and extended à la carte service to be offered to all the other tables in the building. In that event, my hon. and learned Friend would complain to the management and then to the owner. I am here tonight complaining to the owner, having received no satisfaction from the management."

Objecting to proposals by the National Grid to construct new transmission lines in his constituency, despite planning permission, he illustrates his point:

"To make an analogy to what has happened on a more human scale, it is as if I were to propose to my hon. Friend the Minister that I should build a house on a plot adjacent to his house. The plot is well screened and out of sight. He believes that I will be a good neighbour, he raises no objections, planning permission is duly given and I start to build my house. Then I say to him:

"By the way, I need a driveway and the only place I can put it is through your front garden, because no one else will agree to have it. Everyone knows that a house has to have access. Well, everyone knows that a power station has to be linked to the national grid, but it was only after planning permission had been given that it became apparent in my constituency that a £2 million project would be needed and that most of it would pass down the Vale of York."

Complaining about the Minister of Agriculture, Fisheries and Food, the right hon. Nicholas Brown, MP giving way to Europe, Hague says: "The Prime Minister [Tony Blair] accuses us of following an empty-chair policy, but his own small band of Members of the European Parliament have decided this week to boycott Strasbourg, leaving their seats empty as a protest against the French. He accuses us of pursuing an empty-chair policy, but it is never more empty than when the Prime Minister is sitting in it."

Like Denis Healey before him, Hague usually targeted his wit at the big politicians of the day. Tony Blair was a favourite. Hague had ample opportunity to outwit Blair during Prime Minister's Question Time.

In the early days of their encounters Blair usually dismissed Hague's wit and humour, sometimes peevishly, as schoolboy debating points. However, being a consummate politician, he learned that it was better to acknowledge Hague's genius since Hague always had a robust reply. For example:

Blair: "... he is all right dancing around the Dispatch Box with sixth form debating society phrases."

Hague responds: "We always know that, when the Prime Minister gets on to the sixth form debating society, he does not know how to answer the question."

Again Blair says: "Whatever smart debating points the Leader of the Opposition makes in this debate …"

Hague answers again: "Whenever the Prime Minister mentions smart debating points, we know that he has none of his own …"

An example of Hague trying to get Tony Blair to give a clear answer can be seen in this quote from January 1998:

"Two Ministers are engaged in warfare over welfare and everybody at Westminster knows it. It is as good a well-kept secret as a grudge borne by the Chancellor [Gordon Brown]."

After listing disputes between Ministers, e.g. the Minister wants expensive reform, and the Chancellor wants cheap ones; there are opposing opinions within the Cabinet. Hague continues:

"It is no wonder he had to send the Minister without Portfolio to Disney World to ask Mickey Mouse. Has the Prime Minister received any hoax calls from a man claiming to be the Chancellor of the Exchequer and wanting a friendly chat? While he is answering that question will he describe what the Secretary of State for Social Security meant by affluence testing?"

Tony Blair gives an evasive answer that mentions trying to target benefits on those who need them most.

Hague continues: "It is a pretty straightforward question. All we want to know is what the Secretary of State for Social Security meant by affluence testing? Millions of people have read her comments, and take her seriously – God help them

– so millions of people want to know what the phrase means. Does it mean means-testing or does it mean something else?"

Still not satisfied with Tony Blair's answer Hague continues: "We want welfare reform ... What we want to know is when the Government will decide where they are going on welfare reform ... the Secretary of State for Social Security talks about affluence testing, an unnamed Minister briefs the Sunday papers that the Prime Minister has ruled that out and the Deputy Prime Minister [John Prescott] is put in charge of the committee on welfare reform because the Prime Minister thinks that the Chancellor [Gordon Brown] has lost his marbles and cannot be in charge of it. Now the Prime Minister cannot define affluence testing. What is affluence testing and is it an option?"

The Prime Minister reverts to mentioning a few sixth form debating points.

Responding to the Queen's speech of 2000 Hague attacked the Prime Minister's record:

"In more than twenty years in politics, he has betrayed every cause he believed in, contradicted every statement he has made, broken every promise he has given and breached every agreement he has entered into. There is a lifetime of U-turns, errors and sell-outs. All those hon. Members who sit behind the Prime Minister and wonder whether they stand for anything any longer, or whether they defend any principle, know who has led them to that sorry state."

Blair responded by criticising what he saw as Hague's bandwagon politics although he acknowledged that Hague made a very witty, funny speech but it summed up his leadership as: "good jokes, lousy judgement".

While Hague spoke in support of the military action proposed by the Prime Minister during the debate before the 2003 Iraq War one could lip-read Tony Blair saying to his then Foreign Secretary Jack Straw: "He's good, you know."

On a referendum on proportional representation, so beloved by the Liberal Democrats, because it would give them more seats, Hague attacks Tony Blair:

"It is now clear that certain things that the Government committed themselves to in their manifesto will never be enacted in the current Parliament. The Government's manifesto said: 'We are committed to a referendum on the voting system for the House of Commons' and their annual report told us that the referendum was 'on course' so where is it? There is always one group of people gullible enough to believe that the promise of a proportional representation referendum is about to be kept. The Prime Minister promised a proportional representation referendum to the right hon. Member for Yeovil [Paddy Ashdown]. It is all recounted in the thrilling page-turner *The Ashdown Diaries*. Page 276 – not many people have reached page 276 – [Hague quotes from the book] '4th September 1994, Blair: You must understand that I am not playing a tactical manoeuvre on you. You can trust me on this! Ashdown: I said I believed him.'

"It is touching really, is it not? More recently, the right hon. Member for Yeovil, now older and wiser, well older anyway, when asked by friends whether the Prime Minister had played him for a fool sighed and replied: 'He was sincere at the time.'

"That is the trouble with the Prime Minister. He can be sincere about something at the time he is asked, but he is sincere about the opposite the next time he is asked. The Liberal Democrats are all still sitting there … eager beavers, waiting for a Proportional Representation commitment from Labour at the next election and willing again to believe it. It just shows that the Government cannot fool all the people all the time, but they can fool all the Liberal Democrats most of the time."

When Tony Blair changed the arrangement for Prime Minister's Question Time from two 15-minute sessions to one half-hour session Hague gives his opinion as follows:

"Prime Minister Tony Blair announced a change in the procedures for his own Question Time without so much as a nod, request or acknowledgement in the direction of the rest of the house … to ensure that the questions put to him in the House are more easily predictable."

On 24 June 2009, in a debate on the inquiry into the war in Iraq, Hague said that there was genuine disappointment that the Prime Minister had produced proposals for such a secretive, behind-closed-doors inquiry, accentuated by the fact that only the previous week the Prime Minister had talked of improving accountability and transparency. Hague continues with one of his graphic illustrations:

"Since then the Government have engaged in a series of climb-downs – a U-turn that was executed in stages as painful to watch as those of a learner driver doing a six-point turn having started off the wrong way down a motorway."

Hague complained frequently that Tony Blair did not answer the questions put to him at Prime Minister's Question Time.

In 1998 he says: "I am not surprised that the Prime Minister asks for up to two weeks' notice of questions on the internet, as we have never known him to answer them live."

In 2001 Hague says: "In the last year I have asked the right hon. Gentleman 20 questions on health and answers we have had zero; 23 on crime, answers zero; 38 on tax and the economy, answers zero."

William Hague argues that the waiting list to see a consultant has doubled since Tony Blair became Prime Minister.

Blair gives a brief answer but not quite to the point.

Hague replies: "It is a good job that there is not a waiting list for a straight answer, or we would be here for a very long time indeed."

Attacking Tony Blair on a Budget leak from the Treasury to the *Financial Times* Hague asks: "Is he aware that Hugh Dalton, the Labour Chancellor who resigned over a Budget leak – admittedly, he was old Labour and one could trust him – said that one must always own up?"

Re. tax on pension funds:

"Finally, I congratulate the Prime Minister on his role as a film producer. It is touching that he took so much trouble to make a film celebrating our world-class industries, entrepreneurial economy, consumer choice and flexible labour markets, all of which were created by Conservative Governments.

"Does he recall being asked on the same day: 'Will Labour tax pension funds?' Does he recall replying, also in the *Evening Standard*: 'Our public expenditure plans require no extra taxation.'?

"Now the right hon. Gentleman has clobbered pension funds with £5 billion of extra taxation a year, does he agree that he misled millions of future pensioners as well as future students?

"Does the Prime Minister recall being asked by the *Evening Standard* during the election campaign 'Will Labour introduce fees for higher education?'

"Does he recall replying: 'Labour has no plans to introduce tuition fees for higher education.'?

"Does he regret that now?"

Again: "It is no good the Prime Minister giving the answers he prepared last week to the questions he is being asked this week."

"The Prime Minister finds it difficult to tell the truth about many matters, however trivial. Three years ago, he confided to Des O'Connor that when he was fourteen, he stowed away on a plane from Newcastle to the Bahamas. In 1969, the only exotic destinations served by Newcastle were Jersey and the Isle of Man."

Hague continues:

"In an interview with a local radio station in 1997,

the Prime Minister spoke of his passion for football and reminisced about watching his favourite Newcastle player, centre forward Jackie Milburn, from a seat behind one of the goals at St. James' Park. There are two problems with that statement: seats were not installed behind the goals until the 1990s and Jackie Milburn left the club when the Prime Minister was four years old.

"The Prime Minister was at it again last week when he told listeners at the rock station Heart FM that his favourite tune was 'Where the Streets Have No Name' by U2; when he appeared on *Desert Island Discs*, it was Samuel Barber's 'Adagio for Strings' and Francisco Tarrega's 'Recuerdos de la Alhambra'."

Tony Blair's breaking election promises was a popular theme for William Hague. Regarding the Budget in March 1998 Hague says:

"Before the election, the Prime Minister said: 'We have no plans to increase tax at all.' He told Radio 4 listeners last January: 'The programme of the Labour Party does not imply any tax increases at all.' He told BBC1 viewers four days later: 'There are no hidden tax rises.'

"Two months after they took office, the Labour Government tore up those solemn promises and introduced 17 new tax rises in their first budget."

When the Prime Minister stands at the Dispatch Box and says that pensions will not be hit by a new tax, or that waiting lists are down or that there will be 5,000 extra police, we have to bear in mind that nothing that he says about anything can be relied on. That might be funny when he is talking about tunes, food and childhood memories but when he is talking about taxes, waiting lists … he is seeking to debase and destroy the currency of political discourse in this country."

On cuts to spending on the NHS Hague says:

"The Prime Minister's answer bore so little resemblance to the truth that he could probably get a job in his own press office before long."

Another swipe at rising taxes:

"Every day, step by step, it is clear that this is the Government of the nanny state. This is the Government who tell people how to live. We see it again in the Budget. They tell people: Don't drink, don't smoke, don't hunt, don't have a pension, don't eat beef on the bone, don't save, don't drive a car; if you drive a car, don't park it. The Prime Minister preaches to people about what they should and should not do. This Budget and the last one represent the collection plate being passed around after the sermon."

William Hague quotes the chairman of the Police Federation saying that reductions in police numbers in the past eighteen months have left some communities with no policing at all and produced a sense of disorder and anarchy in some inner city areas.

William Hague questions: "Why does the Prime Minister think he said that?"

The Prime Minister's answer is not to the point so Hague continues:

"So the Prime Minister does not understand why the Police Federation says that. He is meant to be able to cope with these situations now. His office sent a memo around the civil service, a report on which says: 'Rattled Tony Blair has caused fury in Whitehall by issuing new orders to civil servants to stop William Hague making a fool of him in the Commons'. The memo from his private secretary says that the lines to take prepared for the Prime Minister 'are often unusable and the facts are wrong'. Well, we have been telling him that for years and nothing has changed."

Commenting on Frank Field's statement that fraud is so serious no Minister 'tells the public the scale', Hague comments that fraud is now up to £7 billion continuing:

"The Prime Minister ought to know that because, after all his broken promises, fraud should be his special subject; he should know about these things."

Sometimes the simplest comments are the best. A master of quotations regarding Blair, Hague says:

"Even the schoolgirls yesterday saw straight through the right hon. Gentleman. As we read in this morning's press one girl covered her head with her pullover as Mr Blair rambled on about devolution. One wrinkled her nose and said: 'He's a big crook.' No wonder they made it a beacon school."

On a controversial £1 million donation from Bernie Ecclestone, Tony Blair answers Ann Widdecombe:

"I would just point out to the hon. Lady that we returned the donation. We refused more donations from Mr Ecclestone."

Hague asks: "When was the £1 million given back to Mr Ecclestone?"

Blair answers: "We have said that we will give the money back. We have already made arrangements to do so … and it will be done in the next few days."

Hague: "The Prime Minister has just told my right hon. Friend [Ann Widdecombe] that the money had been returned. Are we to understand, five minutes into Question Time, that his first answer was not correct?"

On European integration and the Prime Minister saying one thing in one place and something else in another, Hague asks:

"Is that greater integration something that the Prime Minister welcomes? If it is, why does he not say so, instead of running around Europe giving more false impressions than Rory Bremner?"

On tax harmonising in Europe when Oskar Lafontaine is quoted as saying that "our British colleagues have asked us not to use the word harmonisation but co-ordination", Hague comments:

"There is nothing anti-European about believing that we should decide our taxes here in the House of Commons. The truth is that the right hon. Gentleman now has to ask the

Germans to use a different word. He has become the Basil Fawlty of Europe. Every time he meets a German, he goes around saying 'Don't mention tax harmonisation'."

Hague complains that the Prime Minister broke his promise on assisted places in schools – just like the promises on waiting lists, class sizes, taxes, tuition fees, grammar schools and junior doctors.

"When it comes to broken promises, he is now for the many and not the few." [a reference to Labour's much trumpeted promise prior to election]

Hague has more to come. On the rise in class sizes he gives figures to support his statement. "He promised smaller class sizes in all classes to the whole country. It is even written on one of his famous mugs. I will show him one; it says: Smaller Class Sizes. It does not say that for five, six and seven year olds [interruption] I know that he wants to see the back of his mugs, but he will have to wait for the reshuffle – [interruption]"

Madam Speaker intervenes saying: "Order, I want to see the mug and hear what the right hon. Gentleman is saying."

Hague answers: "All that the mug says on the bottom is: This product needs warm soapy water. When the Prime Minister publishes the Government's annual report next week, will he skip the warm soapy water and explain to people on this, as on so many other things, he has broken his election promise."

Again: "These questions are about the integrity of the Government. Is it not part of the Prime Minister's job to set standards of truthfulness and integrity for the Government? Is that not what he spectacularly fails to do? He says that waiting lists are down when they are up, that class sizes are down when they are up and that taxes are down when they are up. Now he says that police numbers are up when they are down. Is it not time that he looked around the Cabinet table and was tough on lies and tough on the causes of lies." [a reference to Tony Blair's much trumpeted election promise: Tough on crime and tough on the causes of crime]

On the Government voting for "yet another of the Prime Minister's stealth taxes", which would hit IT companies and drive them to set up businesses abroad, Hague says: "Their effect would be to kill the enterprise culture [by] driving thousands of IT businesses out of this country."

"The Prime Minister is not only economical with the truth, but less than truthful about economics. He has raided pension funds to a greater extent than Robert Maxwell or anyone ever in history ..."

"There is no point posing with a computer every other week trying to be computer-friendly – presumably looking for the on switch."

Complaining that one faction in the Cabinet wants to join the euro now and another faction want to keep it quiet and join by stealth, Hague asks a question:

"When will the Prime Minister get a grip and ... stop his Cabinet Ministers fighting like ferrets in a sack?"

Continuing on the chaos on the euro that Hague says

is spelled out in a memo written by Tony Blair's chief guru, Philip Gould:

"It reads: From Philip to Alastair, Once again Tony Blair is pandering, lacking conviction, unable to hold a position for more than a few weeks; lacking the guts to be able to tough it out … [interruption] Hon. Members should listen; the Labour Party spent a lot of money on that advice. It says: Tony Blair lacks conviction, he's all spin and presentation; he just says things to please people not because he believes them. Tony Blair has not delivered. He is out of touch.

"Does Tony Blair agree with that, or is it just the rest of us?"

Hague was well able to mock the weak aspects of Tony Blair's control over his party. In a debate on the Queen's speech in Labour's second term Hague begins:

"It is a delight to congratulate both members on their speeches, all the more so because they have both refused to use the script set out in the wonderful 'New Labour, New Britain' briefing on the Queen's speech for Labour Members that was so helpfully faxed to my office earlier today. It has an extremely useful model speech insert for hon. Members to use. We all look forward to seeing who makes that speech. The speech does, however, require hon. Members to insert the right name of their constituency – so look out for that pitfall. He continues to show how Members are to refer to improvements in schools, hospitals, employment etc."

After paying tributes to Australia, Hague continues to question Blair:

"Australians are straightforward people, so let me ask the Prime Minister a straightforward question. Does he remember announcing a new Government policy last Friday, to a chorus of derision – something that he must be getting used to these days? In what was billed as a major announcement, he said that drunken and violent thugs would be picked up by the police, taken to a cash point and asked to pay an on-the-spot fine. Can he tell the House which person in the Government came up with that brilliant idea?"

Blair evades the question by pointing out that a fixed penalty notice might be better.

Hague continues: "If there were a fixed penalty notice for evading the question, the right hon. Gentleman would be bankrupt by now."

Blair on William Hague's last Prime Minister's Question Time:

"I want to say that Members on both sides of the House wish him well and good luck for the future. We shall all miss his wit and humour – although I may not, as I was the object of most of it."

Hague said that debating with Blair at the Dispatch Box had been exciting, fascinating, fun, an enormous challenge and, "from my point of view, wholly unproductive in every sense. I am told that in my time at the Dispatch Box I have asked the Prime Minister 1,118 direct questions, but no one has counted the direct answers – it may not take long."

Hague complaining that the Government is not taking responsibility for the shortcomings in the introduction of AS levels says:

"AS level students are told that if they do not offer an adequate attempt to answer the question or complete the task they will be ungraded. It is a good job that the Prime Minister is not doing AS levels."

Shortly after Labour's 1997 election win Tony Blair appointed as Lord Chancellor his old boss at law, the right hon. Lord Irvine of Lairg. The Lord Chancellor soon entered the consciousness of the nation by the inordinately expensive refurbishment of his apartments with graphic illustrations of designer wallpapers in the newspapers. The press had a field day illustrating this expense, particularly as it was deemed to be out of line with Labour's ethos. The situation was not lost on William Hague who could utilise some of the more lurid claims in his altercations with Tony Blair. For example:

"When the Lord Chancellor says that the Human Rights Bill will lead to a privacy law, does the Prime Minister accept his judgement?"

Blair answers no, and proffers an explanation. Hague pursues the matter.

"The Lord Chancellor … said that in black and white … It is here; he can have a look at it. There are endless comments on the matter from the Lord Chancellor. There are enough comments on it from the Lord Chancellor for him to paper his apartment with them. Even the Home Secretary [Jack Straw] is laughing at that. Does the Prime Minister think that the Lord Chancellor was wrong?"

Blair: "No ... I suspect that the Home Secretary was laughing at the right hon. Gentleman and not with him."

Hague: "The Home Secretary laughs with me more often than the Prime Minister would like to think."

As the debate continues Hague adds: "… it is time that the Prime Minister stopped dithering and made up his mind. The Lord Chancellor could have sorted it out ages ago if he were not so busy flicking through furniture catalogues."

Referring to the government's top priority to reduce spending on welfare reform Hague continues:

"However, it is now clear that Labour came to power with a heap of promises, a bundle of aspirations, a lorry-load of clichés but nothing resembling a plan the policy looks at first sight — from what the Chancellor has said today — as if it will cost the taxpayer a great deal more, will be a disincentive to work for thousands of people and will mean that hundreds of thousands of women will see more than £50 a week taken from their purses and placed into their partners' wallets.

"It means that the Chancellor has done a botched DIY job on welfare reform, at a price that the Lord Chancellor's decorators would have been proud of."

Re. Labour's Paymaster General, Geoffrey Robinson MP having £12 million in offshore trusts:

"The Chancellor's next betrayal was in his so-called crusade against tax avoidance. We notice that the Paymaster General could not bear to be here to listen to the announcements. This is the Government who appointed as the Minister responsible for offshore tax trusts and tax avoidance a man with offshore tax trusts who influences them and is presumably in charge of implementing today's changes to them. That is breathtaking hypocrisy. We shall judge today's changes in tax law against this simple test – the Robinson test. Will the Paymaster General continue to escape tax after today's changes? Will the Minister for tax avoidance continue to avoid tax? We suspect that he may, and that despite all the pre-election rhetoric and the Chancellor's reforms today, the Swiss bank family Robinson will stay in business and out of tax."

Another swipe at Geoffrey Robinson, the Paymaster General:

"What happened to the Freedom of Information Bill that was to be in the Queen's speech? Nothing seems more ridiculous than ... the Paymaster General, who has woven such a web of secrecy around his affairs that no one understands how he borrowed a fiver from Robert Maxwell and came back years later as a multi-millionaire."

On how the Prime Minister has surrounded himself with cronies:

"They are indeed feather-bedding, pocket-lining, money-grabbing cronies. The Prime Minister has created a culture of cronyism in which the Paymaster General hangs on to his job because he has villas in high places, and in which Ministers do not even blush when they try to make the wife of his private pollster the deputy chairman of the BBC."

This was a reference to reports that Tony Blair and family made frequent use of free accommodation provided by rich politicians.

De-bunking the pompous is child's play for William Hague. Peter Mandelson provided ripe opportunities. Mandelson, friend of Tony Blair and one-time enemy of Gordon Brown, was surprisingly recalled to government by Brown when he was Prime Minister to revive the fortunes of the Labour Party for the 2010 general elections. Mandelson had been given unprecedented privileges by way of compensation by Tony Blair when he had to resign from previous ministerial appointments.

Hague comments:

"Lord Mandelson, whom I believe we must now deferentially refer to as the First Secretary ... In mentioning Lord Mandelson, I did not mean to send a chill down the spine of Ministers, but it is now impossible to discuss the operation of Government or Parliament without reference to his opinions. The unelected Prime Minister has managed to produce the most powerful unelected deputy since Henry VIII appointed Cardinal Wolsey – except that Cardinal Wolsey was more sensitive in his handling of colleagues than the noble Lord Mandelson is. His personal retinue of eleven Ministers, six of whom attend him in the House of Lords, is the largest in the Government. The Lord Mandelson ...

has gone around instead collecting titles and even whole departments to add to his name. His title now adds up to 'The right hon. the Baron Mandelson of Foy in the county of Herefordshire and Hartlepool in the county of Durham, First Secretary of State, Lord President of the Privy Council and Secretary of State for Business, Innovation and Skills'. It would be no surprise to wake up in the morning and find that he had become an archbishop [laughter]. That is exactly what happened with Cardinal Wolsey.

"Does he remember announcing a new Government policy last Friday?" Hague continues listing the fears of Labour Ministers and MPs, ending: "and all of them are living in fear of one Minister with a very long title for whom, at the last election, no one in the country ever voted at all."

Regarding the post of High Representative in Europe: Hague congratulates Baroness Ashton on her appointment as High Representative, wishing her well, noting that her appointment was "the outcome of a murky process, to put it mildly". He then says that, "in this age of transparency, democracy and freedom of information, the Minister may wish to shed light on whether it is true that the Prime Minister put forward three names for nomination as High Representative to the European socialist leaders, pointing out that it appeared that Lord Mandelson (he of the multiple titles) was put forward … Ministers now have the opportunity to deny that if it was not the case" [i.e. if Lord Mandelson's name was not put forward]. He continues, "There is an icy stillness on the Government benches. If it is true that, unlike the Foreign Secretary, the First Secretary of State was happy to be nominated as the High Representative, it is an important piece of information that the second most senior member of the Government was happy to depart the Government at this point. This would be not merely a rat leaving the ship, but the Lord High Admiral himself looking for a raft – although we are reluctant to suggest additional titles in case he is tempted to adopt them."

In May 2009:

"Finally, on the question of support, given the widespread reports that the Foreign Secretary is about to be replaced by Lord Mandelson, may I invite him to agree that in the 21st century the appointment by an unelected Prime Minister [Gordon Brown] of an unelected Foreign Secretary in an unelected House would be a very good argument for an immediate general election."

He adds later that if Lord Mandelson succeeded in displacing the Foreign Secretary it would be inappropriate in the 21st century for the British Foreign Secretary not to be a Member of the House of Commons.

Another dig at Mandelson who showed an interest in the good life came on the national loan guarantee scheme to help the economy to recover:

"My party called for a national loan guarantee scheme all the way back to November and the Government have dithered on about it ever since. They are all over the place. The Prime Minister is on his way to Chile. The Business Secretary [Mandelson] has just arrived in Brazil. Should he not be implementing those schemes instead of unpacking his Speedos on a Latin American beach?"

Many MPs and Ministers enjoyed Hague's wit and made this clear from time to time.

Denis MacShane rose. His first point was to agree with the last point William Hague made. He then added:

"We always enjoy the Mandelson speech from the Shadow Foreign Secretary – I hope there is a lot more of it to come …"

Regarding high Labour council taxes in Sedgefield – the Prime Minister's constituency – in fact the thirteenth highest council tax in Band D, at £967, Hague says that the Prime Minister is in good company on the Government benches – with Hartlepool at £978, "no wonder the right hon. Member for Hartlepool [Mandelson] always keeps a posh house in London."

On the same topic Hague compliments David Miliband on not accepting the post of High Representative in Europe:

"In any event, his decision shows laudable tenacity or appropriate faith in the nation state or a conviction that, whatever happens, the Prime Minister will soon be gone."

There was much speculation that David Miliband hoped to be the next Prime Minister.

John Prescott, MP for Hull, was a natural target for Hague. Cheerful, sunny and somewhat corpulent he was the epitome of good living. He was proud of his working class background; he had been a seaman. He lived in style, owning two Jaguars, hence he became known as "Two Jags".

He is also well remembered for throwing a hearty punch at a protester who hit him with an egg. He was Deputy Prime Minister. He was once photographed playing croquet during working hours and had to answer his critics. In answer to Prescott's statement about the Olympics in Beijing, Hague makes reference to this:

"If the right hon. Gentleman gets to the Olympics, will he convey the message from all parties that we are proud to have the 2012 Olympics in this country? Will he respond to the deep disappointment on both sides of the House that he will not take part in either the boxing or the croquet, which used to be an Olympic sport, particularly bearing in mind law 1(c) of the rules of Oxford croquet – when a player has scored enough points, he is officially described as 'pegged out' and has to be removed from the game? Would it not be fairer to the British taxpayer if he were now removed from the game?"

Prescott makes a robust reply saying that the croquet set was provided by the ex-Chancellor Ken Clarke (Conservative): "I know a lot was made of it being during working hours, but I notice that there are not many people here today during working hours. Perhaps some are at Ascot, and the *Daily Mail* will be there photographing them ..."

Prescott was also Secretary of State for Transport and the Regions as well as Environment. Prescott's transport White Paper with powers to restrain traffic by electronic charging would harm those on low incomes. The Bill proposed congestion charges, motorway taxes and car parking taxes on top of more rises in fuel taxes and road taxes.

Hague comments on the Transport Bill's effect on car drivers:

"To Mondeo man, once so cherished by New Labour's spin doctors, it is another kick in the teeth. People work hard and save hard to own a car. They do not want to be told that they cannot drive it by a Deputy Prime Minister whose idea of a Park and Ride scheme is to park one Jaguar so that he can ride away in another."

Later he comments, again on Prescott:

"On Monday, the Deputy Prime Minister, who is not here – presumably his bus is late – told school-run mothers, people struggling home with their weekly shopping and people living in the countryside that they were making unnecessary journeys. He then jumped into his car and was driven 200 yards to the office."

Commenting on the Government's annual report that stated: "Integrated transport policy – done!" Hague gives his assessment:

"Done. The Government actually think that they have done it, but the only thing the Deputy Prime Minister [Prescott] has integrated is a chicken masala with an afternoon nap."

Commenting on Prescott being given the job of reviewing the competition in airports:

"He is presumably in the Maldives, examining how they integrate their transport strategy. Looking at how to integrate sunbathing with water-skiing will come in handy in Hull."

Another swipe at Prescott about the 12 per cent rise in diesel duties and the problems of jobs lost in the road haulage industry:

"... while the Deputy Prime Minister who has responsibility for transport was chasing angel fish around a coral reef."

After a jibe at Prescott for being "busy doing nothing" as Secretary of State for the Environment, Transport and the Regions when his areas did not get much mention in the Queen's Speech:

"Judging by the content of the Queen's Speech, it is probably the last Queen's Speech of the current Parliament. In fact there was so little in it that I think it was very good of Her Majesty to come down to deliver it at all." [The Queen's Speech is provided by the Prime Minister.]

Hague continues his comments on Prescott:

"He has never been one for nursing a grievance quietly so he can tell us all about it whenever he wants.

"At least people with a Jaguar can breathe a sigh of relief that the right hon. Gentleman's crazy anti-car proposals are stuck in a lay-by. Those with two Jags can breathe two sighs of relief."

Continuing his attack on Prescott saying that the Deputy Prime Minister came second in the league of incompetence, that he has had a vintage year, quoting a gaffe by Prescott:

"The Green Belt is a Labour achievement and now we are going to build on it."

Hague continues: "The right hon. Gentleman was standing in at Prime Minister's Question Time so much that Wednesday is now the only day that the Prime Minister spends in this country."

He continued:

"As Lady Richard revealed recently, the Deputy Prime Minister has even been chairing Cabinet meetings. She says in her diary for a Cabinet meeting on 19th June: 'Blair said he was in favour of the Millennium Dome and then disappeared, leaving John Prescott in charge. The meeting fell apart'."

Again Hague attacks Prescott: "Will the Deputy confirm that despite the initiative on departmental efficiency savings, he has managed to spend £645 changing the sign outside his office from 'Office of the Deputy Prime Minister' to 'Deputy Prime Minister's Office'? Does not that symbolise the shocking waste of money under this Government when thousands of jobs are being cut from the NHS?"

On mention of Prescott as big hitter, Prescott rose and Hague said: "Steady, I do judo."

Prescott could be generous. On Hague standing down as leader of the Conservative party Prescott replies:

"As for the speech of the right hon. Member for Richmond, Yorkshire [Hague], the Leader of the Opposition, may I tell him that it was a vintage Hague performance? It was extraordinarily witty and eloquent, which is what we expect of him."

Gordon Brown was Chancellor of the Exchequer for all of Tony Blair's time as Prime Minister, thought to be because this was the job he wanted and Blair did not have the courage or the power to move him down. Brown was a perfect target for Hague, being of a gloomy demeanour and displaying little sense of humour.

In a debate on the budget Hague attacks:

"As ever, the most interesting thing about what the Chancellor said was what he did not say. He did not say – but it is the truth – that the total tax burden will rise next year as a result of his cumulative decisions. He did not say – but it is the truth – that, as a result of his decisions in three budgets, this is the third year running in which we will have higher taxes because of the decisions of this Government ... After three years in a row he gets to keep that reputation [for higher taxes] forever ... The Chancellor said that the Budget is good for families. It is good for families who do not have a mortgage, who are not married, who do not run a car, who do not smoke and who do not save for a pension. For a family like that the Budget is fine. There may even be a family like that somewhere in the country: it sounds suspiciously like the Chancellor to me."

A reference to the much-publicised feud between Blair and Brown, on the birth of Blair's son:

"For once I begin with congratulations – I congratulate the Prime Minister and his wife on their happy family news.

In future, when the Prime Minister hears the sound of crying in the next room, it will not be the Chancellor wishing that he had his job."

Regarding the post of Prime Minister in Europe:

"The creation of that job took many years and the present Prime Minister feels that it took almost as long to get round to his turn to hold it. To see how the post of a President of the European Council could evolve is not difficult even for the humblest student of politics and it is, of course, rumoured that one Tony Blair may be interested in the job. If that prospect makes us uncomfortable on the Conservative benches, just imagine how it will be viewed in Downing Street.

"We can all picture the scene at a European Council sometime next year. Picture the face of our poor Prime Minister (Gordon Brown) as the name Blair is nominated by one President and Prime after another: the look of utter gloom on his faceat the nauseating, glutinous praise oozing from every head of Government, the rapid revelation of a majority view agreed behind closed doors when he, as usual, was excluded. Never would he more regrand et no longer being in possession of a veto: the famous dropped jaw, almost hitting the floor, as he realises that there is no option but to join in. Then the awful moment when the motorcade of the President of Europe sweeps into Downing Street. The gritted teeth and bitten nails: the Prime Minister emerges from his door with a smile of intolerable anguish, the choking sensation of the words 'Mr President', being forced from his mouth. And then, once in the Cabinet room the melodrama of 'when will you hand over to me' all over again."

Complaining further about the extra taxes imposed by the Chancellor:

"The Chancellor is now posing as the man who likes to distribute a few little goodies ... He is the man you meet in a pub who says: Lend us a fiver and then I'll buy you a drink. He is the pickpocket Chancellor who shakes your hand with a smile after he has stealthily removed your wallet. He is the pickpocket Chancellor, aided and abetted by his next door neighbour [Blair], the artful dodger."

Continuing his complaints, this time, about the Chancellor's stealth tax:

"In 1997, the Chancellor's £5 billion tax on pension funds was described in the pocket guide to the budget as 'other taxes to encourage companies to invest'."

He continues on the Chancellor as a tax-raising Chancellor and outlines a £4.5 billion total of new stealth taxes heading people's way in a few weeks time:

"The Chancellor is like a mugger who grabs someone's money and then wants that person to thank him for providing the bus fare home."

On the Chancellor's statement that the tax burden on the average family will fall to its lowest level for 30 years, Hague explains:

"However, this included only direct taxes and left out all of his stealth taxes on petrol, pensions, cars, alcohol, cigarettes and council tax. His statement was watched by millions of people, and some of them may even have believed it, but it would be true only for people who never drive, never smoke, never drink and do not have a pension or even a local council. In other words it does not apply to anyone in the country."

On the Chancellor taking £5 billion a year raided from pension funds:

"In his Britain, there is no reward for people who do the right thing and save for themselves and their families. It is the double-take economy: you take responsibility and the Government take your money."

Congratulating the Chancellor on his budget in 1997: "On a personal level I congratulate the Chancellor on his fortitude in delivering his speech and doing so within the space of one hour with only the assistance of water."

However, commenting on the fact that the UK had built up more than £650 billion in pension funds:

"It is a smash and grab raid on pension funds in this country. The Chancellor is using environmental taxes as another vehicle by which to raise the tax burden overall ... He calls it a green budget, but it is actually still a red budget which increases taxes on the people of this country."

Prophetic comment:

"The Chancellor should be warned that the real judgements on the Budget will be passed over the years to come. In future years we will want to know what the Government have done with the best economic inheritance in decades. They had better be ready to be held to account for that."

On budget figures, 7th March 2001:

"It is a good thing that it is the Chancellor and not the Prime Minister who is giving the budget – we might even get some figures out of the organ grinder that we do not get from the monkey."

Speaking about the death of Donald Dewar, a man of lugubrious countenance:

"He was a cultured, accomplished, civilised, extremely entertaining and endearing man ... he had a happy melancholy about him ... It was once written about him that he was happy only when he was thoroughly depressed."

Hague points out a good example of the double-speak of politicians when congratulating the Member for Aberavon [Sir James Morris] who had been a Member of Parliament continuously for 41 years:

"He once said 'I don't regard myself as a professional politician', which is quite a statement for someone who has been Parliamentary Secretary, Minister of Transport; Parliamentary Secretary, Minister of Power; Minister of Defence (Equipment); Secretary of State for Wales; shadow spokesman on legal affairs; Attorney-General; served in the Cabinets of three Prime Ministers; and spent 33 years on the front bench of the House of Commons. With that record, he would have to be a professional politician to claim that he was not one."

Hague looks at another surprising event:

Yesterday Opposition front bench members came to the House to defend the statuarysick pay system, the establishment of which they opposed ten years ago. They have opposed every change to it. There they sit, gloomy, a range of exhausted volcanoes, unable to come up with any ideas for the future, having privatised that activity and farmed it out to the Commission for Social Justice."

Then, another graphic illustration of an opponent who could not clarify an issue on the Statutory Sick Pay Bill:

"It was rather less like going off a road and into a field than going round an endlessly confusing roundabout, with many signals pointing in different directions and with the hon. Gentleman at the wheel of the car, careering around the roundabout, peering into the distance, looking for something that would come over the horizon which would present a more attractive target than the Bill before the House at the time. He ought to reflect on some of his comments in that speech."

On Welsh Affairs and the readiness of Labour to sign anything that comes from Brussels:

"I sometimes get the impression that opposition Members would sign any piece of paper that floated across the English Channel."

On investment into Wales he answers Mr Marshall:

"My hon. Friend is right – and he made his point so well that he even drew a cheer from the hon. Member for

Bolsover [Dennis Skinner – the Beast of Bolsover]. That must be something of a first in this context."

Re. Scotland and Wales Bill:

"The Secretary of State for Scotland said that the Bill was a modest measure ... He said that it was modest because it was short, but not everything that is short is modest, otherwise there would be much more modesty in the Chamber."

Clarifying the use of language: "Under the previous Government, more and additional meant the same thing, as they usually do in the English language. More than there are now."

On vandals rioting in the City and groups defacing the Cenotaph, answering an accusation that he was exploiting the situation, Hague answers: "But he is not the one who went down to the Cenotaph yesterday, peeled an onion and said it can never happen again – had already happened twice."

On the Government piling extra taxes and regulations on businesses, the number of employees in manufacturing in Great Britain having fallen by 206,000 since the General election and complaining of £10 billion for red tape and regulation asking:

"Why is what Lord Haskins said, for example, that entrepreneurs are being distracted ... from growing their businesses by the cumulative burden of taxation and ... regulation not written in that folder that he is always consulting? There must be something in that folder other than, if pressed, waffle for as long as you can."

A pertinent comment at the time:

"This Government cannot even tell the truth about the duty on a litre of petrol. They are so busy with trivia such as banning musical chairs, bailing out the Dome, telling the royal family to move house and counting the number of fat people on television that they have forgotten what really matters to people in this country."

Always able to make a jovial, off-the-cuff retort, for example, when Denis McShane thanked William Hague for destroying his career, Hague responded:

"The hon. Gentleman does not need me to destroy his career when he can open his mouth at any time."

Comments on David Miliband were generally positive. Miliband was the bright young star of the Labour Party, rumoured to be agitating to become leader after Tony Blair.

Hague apologised for making some points to Miliband, the Foreign Secretary, "because he is perfectly good at consultation with the opposition". He continues:

"Clearly he was misinformed and not properly briefed by a Downing Street that does not share his willingness to consult on and agree matters with the Opposition. Let us hope that that emboldens him when he comes to his next opportunity to depose the Prime Minister, which normally recurs about every twelve weeks."

One word is often enough:

"The cut in corporation tax which, according to the Red Book, gives businesses £700 million in two years' time. Other changes in corporation tax, which the Chancellor glided over in his speech, will cost businesses £2,000 million in the same year. That is in the Red Book – or, in the Prime Minister's case, the unread book."

Arguing that beef-on-the-bone regulations are absurd:

"It is no good hiding behind the chief medical officer ... The institute of Trading Standards Administration says that the government have left it to enforce the unenforceable. With a legal touch like that, it is no wonder that the Prime Minister [Tony Blair] gave up the Bar for politics – unlike the Minister of Agriculture, Fisheries and Food who sometimes gives up politics for the bar."

Responding to the Queen's speech:

"It is a happier tradition at the opening of this debate that the Leader of the Opposition congratulates the hon. Members who proposed and seconded the Loyal Address. I can do that without reservation today. Traditionally the Government ask one bright, rising Member of the House, who they hope will be helpful in the future, and one old-timer who has been sporadically helpful in the past. They have done that on this occasion.

"The hon. and learned Member for Edinburgh, Pentlands [Dr Clark] made a good speech. She was first elected to the House last year. She is one of only seven female Queen's Counsels in Scotland – a mark of her great distinction, which she displayed this afternoon. I had to delve quite deeply into her impressive CV to find its highlight, which was that she represented her university at ice dancing. She might reflect on the fact that skating on thin ice and going to the Bar are ideal preparations for being a Member of Parliament."

A jovial look at himself:

"Will he agree that being interested in sport helps one to keep life in perspective? As I reminded someone the other day, I support Rotherham United at football, Wales at rugby and Yorkshire at cricket. When one supports those teams, the result of the general election is just a minor irritation."

Statement on the G8 summit in Birmingham, 1998:

Regarding recent blunders in the Foreign Office, domain of Robin Cook:

"Is not the Foreign Office being run like a Dad's Army outfit, by a Foreign Secretary who combines the pompousness of Captain Mainwaring, the incompetence of Private Pike and the calm of Corporal Jones?

On the question of Britain joining the euro, 1999:

"Labour want to keep the options open, the Conservatives are against joining the euro. The Italian Treasury Minister is quoted as saying 'We have all agreed that the less we talk about the euro the better'."

Hague continues: "He must have been in charge of the Labour Party's election campaign."

Compliment from a colleague: "The hon. Member for Glasgow South West has gone. I was about to address his point. So much for his enthusiasm for an answer! ... The hon. Gentleman wants to intervene for a third time. I will let him do so once again."

Mr Davidson returns asking: "Will the Foreign Secretary give way?"

Hague answers, "The hon. Gentleman has returned. I will give way to him so that he can nip out again while I answer his question."

Then a compliment to Hague from Davidson:

"In my defence, I came back. I had to leave because I had visitors. I apologise to the right hon. Gentleman for that. I explained to them that the joys of listening to him were greater than those of meeting them. They are not voters in my constituency, which makes it a great deal easier to say that."

Use of numbers effectively:

"We are in many ways pleased that the Foreign Secretary [David Miliband] has stayed in post, because there has been enough ministerial chaos in the Foreign and Commwealth Office. This is a serious point, because it might be thought that a degree of experience, expertise and continuity in the conduct of foreign policy would be a good thing. However, in the two and a half years that the Foreign Secretary has held office, he has gone through fourteen junior Ministers, none of whom has been with him throughout, and there have been twelve European Ministers in twelve years."

McShane: "Thirteen."

Hague: "Oh, there may be a thirteenth."

William Hague could be generous and this mingled well with his humour. On the departure of John Prescott:

"This only goes to show that, for all the harsh words that the right hon. Gentleman and I exchanged over the years politics will be dramatically less entertaining without him. Not only do we not know how the Labour party will manage without him, we do not know how the Conservatives will manage without him. Nevertheless we wish him a thumping good retirement with many years of good humour and good health off the front bench."

William Hague was Secretary of State for Foreign and Commonwealth Affairs 2010–2014.

However, all good things come to an end. Hague's elevation to the role of Foreign Secretary left fewer opportunities for wit. He explains in 2010 that his speech had to be tempered and curtailed. "I explained yesterday that the edge is taken off blunt speaking by becoming Foreign Secretary of the United Kingdom and it is probably in our national interest that the edge is taken off."

On 14 July 2014 William Hague stood down as Secretary of State for Foreign Affairs to become Leader of the House of Commons in preparation for his planned retirement from electoral plolitics. At the 2015 general election he did not put his name forward for re-election. He was elevated as a Life Peer in the 2015 Dissolution Honours List and created Baron Hague of Richmond in the county of North Yorkshire.

Despite his clever, witty comments Hague always retained a superior, restrained and gentlemanly demeanour. He was not just the wittiest but the least predictable, not just in the areas of question but in the angle he took.

There has been no one in Parliament since his resignation who can match his presence or enliven the dullness of the House of Commons.

Printed in Great Britain
by Amazon